Annette Bay Pimentel ✦ Illustrated by Rich Lo

Mountain Chef

How One Man

Lost His Groceries, Changed His Plans, and Helped Cook Up the National Park Service

ini Charlesbridge

D0239561

For Grandad, whose Bryce Canyon story
sent me looking for this one, and, of course, for David—A. B. P.

Dedicated to my parents, who kept the family together
through tough times in a culture and country
they knew very little about—R. L.

Special thanks to Yenyen F. Chan, Park Ranger,
Yosemite National Park, for her invaluable expertise and
for her unflagging patience with my stream of questions—A. B. P.

First paperback edition 2019
Text copyright © 2016 by Annette Bay Pimentel
Illustrations copyright © 2016 by Rich Lo
All rights reserved, including the right of reproduction in whole or in part in any form.
Charlesbridge and colophon are registered trademarks of Charlesbridge Publishing, Inc.

Published by Charlesbridge
85 Main Street
Watertown, MA 02472
(617) 926
www.charlesbridge.com

Library of Congress Cataloging-in-Publication Data
Names: Pimentel, Annette Bay, author. | Lo, Rich, illustrator.
Title: Mountain chef: how one man lost his groceries, changed his plans, and helped
        cook up the National Park Service/Annette Bay Pimentel; illustrated by Rich Lo.
Description: Watertown, MA: Charlesbridge, [2016]
Identifiers: LCCN 2015040753 | ISBN 9781580897112 (reinforced for library use) |
        ISBN 9781580899857 (softcover) | ISBN 9781607348788 (ebook) |
        ISBN 9781607348795 (ebook pdf)
Subjects: LCSH: Sing, Tie—Juvenile literature. | Mather, Stephen Tyng, 1867–1930—
        Juvenile literature. | United States. National Park Service—History—Juvenile
        literature. | Cooks—Biography—Juvenile literature. | Chinese Americans—
        Biography—Juvenile literature. | Camping—California—History—Juvenile
        literature.
Classification: LCC TX649.S494 P56 2016 | DDC 641.5092—dc23 LC record available at
        http://lccn.loc.gov/2015040753

Printed in China
(hc) 10 9 8 7 6 5 4 3 2 1
(sc) 10 9 8 7 6 5 4 3 2 1

Pencil drawings and watercolor washes done on paper,
then scanned and layered in Photoshop
Type set in Estro by Mecanorma
Color separations by Colourscan Print Co Pte Ltd, Singapore
Printed by 1010 Printing International Limited in Huizhou, Guangdong, China
Production supervision by Brian G. Walker
Designed by Susan Mallory Sherman

Tie Sing was a frontier baby, born high in the mountains in Virginia City, Nevada. Growing up, he breathed crisp Sierra air and scuffed through sagebrush. He learned to write in both English and Chinese.

America was a tough place to be Chinese. Bosses paid Chinese workers less than white workers. Townsfolk spat out Chinese names like they'd swallowed river gravel. Most people with Chinese names ended up cooking in restaurants or washing clothes in laundries. Tie Sing, though, had American dirt under his fingernails—and dreams as big as the country he loved. Cramped shacks weren't for him. He made plans— big plans.

He got a job cooking for mapmakers as they tramped through the mountains, naming peaks. With sky for his ceiling and sequoias for his walls, he stirred silky sauces, broiled succulent steaks, and tossed crisp salads. In his sheet-metal oven, he baked sourdough rolls as light as the clouds drifting above the peaks. His reputation grew: the best trail cook in California!

In 1915 Tie Sing got his most important job yet.
A millionaire named Stephen Mather was trying to
convince lawmakers to create a national park service to
protect the country's natural wonders. But in the city,
the roar of business drowned out his talk of mountains
and trees and animals. So Mather invited writers,
tycoons, members of Congress—and even a movie star—
to go camping.

He wanted to show his guests the majesty of America's wild places, but he worried: "Give [a man] a poor breakfast after he has had a bad night's sleep, and he will not care how fine your scenery is." So he bought the best camping gear he could find—newfangled air mattresses for soft and dreamy sleep—and he hired the best trail cook around: Tie Sing.

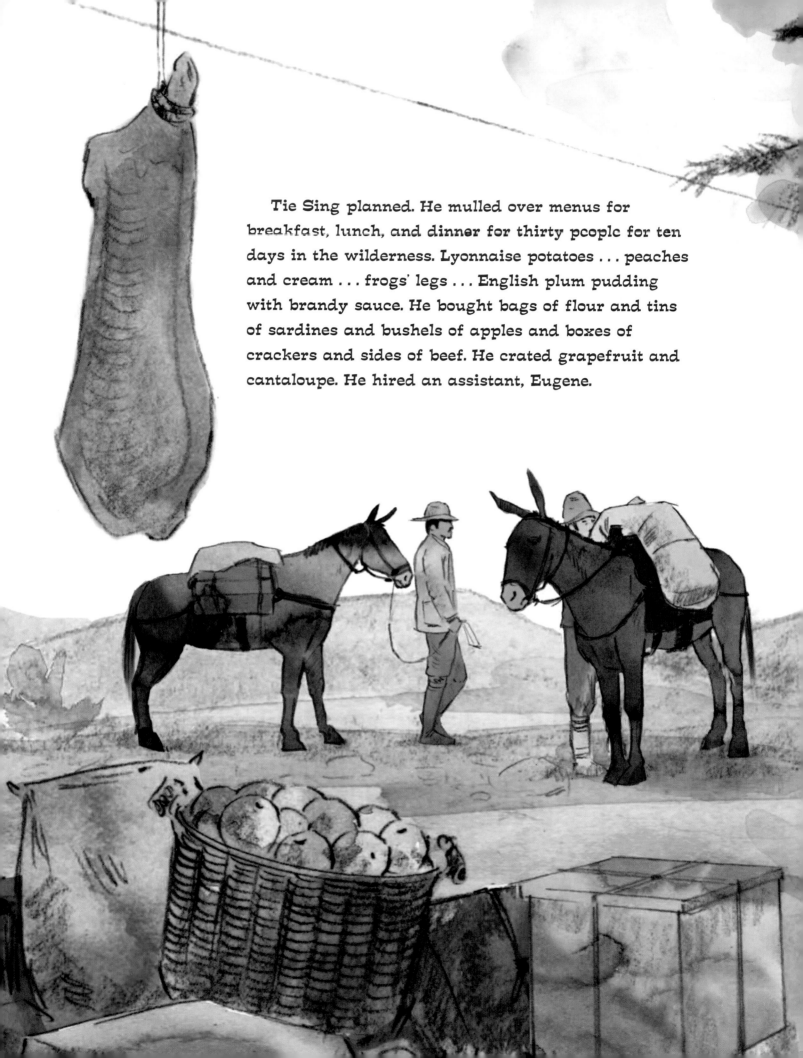

Tie Sing planned. He mulled over menus for breakfast, lunch, and dinner for thirty people for ten days in the wilderness. Lyonnaise potatoes . . . peaches and cream . . . frogs' legs . . . English plum pudding with brandy sauce. He bought bags of flour and tins of sardines and bushels of apples and boxes of crackers and sides of beef. He crated grapefruit and cantaloupe. He hired an assistant, Eugene.

On the trail Mather told stories that made his guests laugh. He scrambled up steep peaks to show them the best views. He plunged with them into mountain pools.

And he counted on Tie Sing to keep everyone comfortable and well fed.

Each morning Tie Sing woke in the shivering dark and whispered instructions to Eugene. They stacked firewood in the cookstoves and fed kindling to trembling flames until the fire burned steady and strong. They watched the edge of the sky turn rosy while they cracked dozens of eggs. As the other campers crawled out of their sleeping bags, Tie Sing packed box lunches and put steaks on to sizzle. He served breakfast as a yellow edge of sun peeked above the horizon.

After breakfast the other campers left to hike to the next campsite. But Tie Sing and Eugene still had work to do. They heated water on the stove and washed the breakfast dishes. They opened the oven doors and stabbed at the ashes to put out the last wisps of flame. Tie Sing mixed a new batch of sourdough.

Then it was time to pack. Tie Sing and Eugene swaddled the china plates, tucked them in a box, and strapped the box to a mule. They folded up the long banquet table. When the ovens were cool enough to take apart, they stacked them neatly and tied them to a mule, too. But first Tie Sing snuggled the sourdough box next to the mule's warm hide, so the dough would rise during the day and be ready by evening to bake up fresh for dinner.

By the time Tie Sing and Eugene trudged off toward the next campsite, the other campers were hours ahead.

Tie Sing and Eugene arrived at the new site just in time to assemble the camp stoves and start a cook fire for dinner. While the oven heated, they washed the heavy linen tablecloth in an icy snowmelt stream and spread it, brighter than white-water foam, over the table. They unpacked the fine china plates and folded thick cloth napkins to cradle the silverware.

Then Tie Sing began to cook. He assembled sardine hors d'oeuvres, sliced juicy cantaloupe, and squeezed lemons to make tart-sweet lemonade. He grilled steaks and venison, fried fish and chicken, and baked sourdough rolls. He served up gourmet meals as fine as any you'd find in a San Francisco restaurant.

Tie Sing knew how to plan.

One morning Tie Sing got a head start on the day by packing his gourmet food before the other campers got up. He strapped it to a mule and then tied the mule in the meadow, where it could munch green grass and purple lupine. He dashed back to the stove to fry another egg and dish up more potatoes. Finally the last camper laid down his napkin, and Tie Sing and Eugene could start the breakfast dishes.

That's when Tie Sing realized that the mule in the meadow had wandered away—with all of the fanciest food on its back! Mather organized the campers to help search. They zigzagged along the river. They crisscrossed the meadow. But the mule had disappeared.

Mather shrugged and set off on the day's hike, but
Tie Sing was so mad he nearly cried. What a disaster!
His carefully planned menus were ruined.

All that day, while he plodded past boulders and wound through sagebrush, he cataloged the food he had left, and dreamed up new menus. He changed his plans.

That night there were no fancy hors d'oeuvres. The food was plain, but the chicken was moist, the gravy velvety, and those sourdough rolls were so light they almost floated up to join the clouds. For dessert Tie Sing baked all-American apple pie.

Mather and the other campers sighed happily as they pushed away from the table. They gathered around the blazing campfire and talked about the stunning scenery they'd seen. They told ghost stories. They made plans for convincing Congress to create a national park service.

After the campers headed off the next day, Tie Sing tied the mules' ropes with extra care. He didn't want another mule wandering away!

The trail along Rattlesnake Creek was narrow and steep. Tie Sing stepped carefully, loose rocks shifting and crunching underfoot. He took it slow, but one mule drifted too close to the edge.

Clatter!

Clang!

Crash!

The mule tumbled off the trail and down the cliff! Boxes burst and bags flew open. Utensils and food flew through the air.

At the bottom the mule shook itself and scrambled back up. It was fine, but the food and gear were not.

At 9:00 that night Tie Sing stumbled into camp with the battered boxes and bent knives and bruised apples he'd salvaged. His sourdough was lost somewhere in the dusty gravel at the bottom of the cliff. No more rolls as light as clouds.

Mather and the other campers had been waiting for hours. They were ravenous. What could Tie Sing feed them? He had to make new plans, and fast!

The food would be simple, but Tie Sing could make sure the setting was elegant. He and Eugene laid china on the linen tablecloth and strung paper lanterns above the table. They stewed those battered apples and baked flat but scrumptious biscuits. That night the campers ate the best applesauce they'd ever tasted.

They ate well the entire trip. But Tie Sing dreamed of more than stuffing hungry bellies. Stephen Mather wasn't the only one who loved the mountains; Tie Sing had the Sierra singing in his blood. He, too, planned to fill the campers with memories.

The last night, for the first time, he didn't hover over the cooking pots. They bubbled on the stove while he bent over tiny slips of paper and wrote in English and Chinese.

After dinner Tie Sing served fortune cookies,
a handwritten message tucked inside each one.

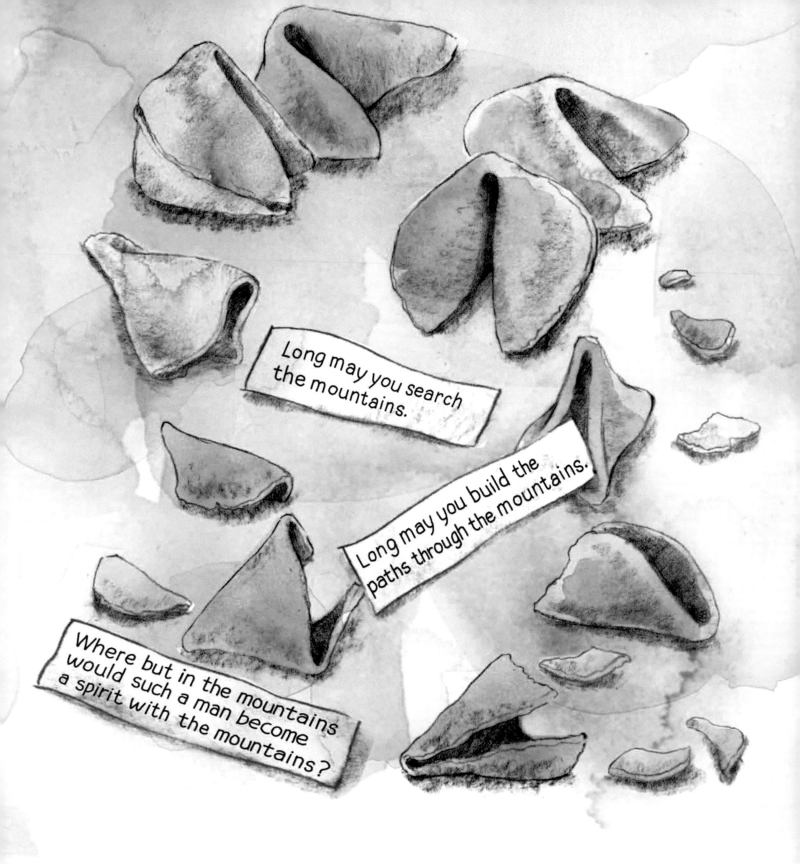

Long may you search the mountains.

Long may you build the paths through the mountains.

Where but in the mountains would such a man become a spirit with the mountains?

The campers read their fortunes and grinned. They would remember the crackle of the campfire and the slant of morning sun across the trail. They would remember dining around the linen tablecloth under the trees.

In the months that followed, they wrote magazine articles, published books, and made movies about America's national parks. On August 25, 1916, exactly one year, one month, and one day after Tie Sing served his fortune cookies, Congress created the National Park Service.

On that day, Tie Sing was on the trail, cooking up more mountain magic.

Today, if you visit Yosemite National Park, you can hike to Sing Peak. It was named for Tie Sing, a mountain-loving American who knew how to plan.

What You May Be Wondering

Courtesy of the Bancroft Library, University of California, Berkeley, 1954.19 Pic

Was Tie Sing real?

Yes! Campers snapped photos of him and wrote admiringly about how he planned for and prepared gourmet meals in the wilderness.

I failed, though, to find any official documents about Tie Sing's life. Francis Farquhar (pronounced *FAR-kwar*), who camped with Tie Sing in 1916, wrote that the trail cook was born in Virginia City, Nevada, but that his birth certificate was destroyed by fire. In Virginia City I learned that the October 1875 fire that leveled most of the town had not touched its birth records. Hopeful, I examined decades of birth certificates but didn't find Tie Sing's.

The county clerk explained to me that births did not legally need to be recorded in Nevada until 1911. Few children born in Virginia City before then had birth certificates.

Farquhar also reports that Tie Sing worked for the United States Geological Survey (USGS) as a trail cook for thirty years. Unfortunately, the USGS has no record of him as an employee because he was a seasonal worker.

Tie Sing was killed in a mountain accident in 1918, while cooking for the USGS. The 10,552-foot Sing Peak in Yosemite National Park and Sierra National Forest bears his name.

Was Tie Sing an American?

Yes! Tie Sing lived during a time of terrible discrimination against ethnic Chinese in the United States. In 1882 Congress passed the Chinese Exclusion Act, which prohibited Chinese people from entering the country. It was the first time that any racial or ethnic restrictions were placed on immigration. The act also declared that Chinese-born people already in the United States would never be allowed to become citizens.

Later, laws became even stricter. Chinese residents had to carry certificates proving their right to be in the country. They could not testify in US courts, even if they were victims of crime.

None of these rules should have applied to Tie Sing, since he was born in the United States and so was automatically an American citizen— but being of Chinese descent and carrying a Chinese name were enough to strip citizens of their rights. In 1895 Wong Kim Ark, who had been born in San Francisco, tried to return to California after a trip abroad. Officials barred his re-entry, saying that since he was ethnically Chinese, he was not a US citizen. His case went all the way to the Supreme Court, which finally decided in 1898 that Wong Kim Ark and other ethnic Chinese born in the United States—like Tie Sing—were in fact US citizens.

Despite the discrimination Tie Sing faced throughout his life, his patriotism impressed his fellow campers. Farquhar wrote that he was "regarded by those who knew him as a fine American."

How did Tie Sing keep the meat from going bad without ice or refrigeration?

Every morning before leaving camp, Tie Sing soaked newspaper in water and then wrapped it around the meat. As he traveled through the arid landscape, the water evaporated, lowering the temperature of the meat.

Early in the trip, the campers shot a deer, so Tie Sing carried venison steaks as well as the beef and chicken he had brought from town. The campers also fished, and Tie Sing used the fresh fish in his meals. Camper Emerson Hough later wrote that if you positioned yourself just right, you could hook a fish and pull it out so that it would go directly into Tie Sing's frying pan.

Why was a national park service important?

In 1872 Yellowstone was declared the first national park. In 1911 President William Howard Taft recommended the formation of a national park service, but he failed to whip up enough enthusiasm among members of Congress. By 1915 there were eleven national parks—but no system of administering the parks.

In January 1915 Stephen Mather was appointed assistant secretary of the interior by President Woodrow Wilson. Mather was

determined both to protect the national parks and to share them with all Americans. Appalled at the bureaucratic red tape in Washington, DC, he dreamed up a camping trip that would change hearts and minds.

Where did they camp?

The Mather Mountain Party started their camping trip in Giant Forest in Sequoia National Park on July 15, 1915. From there, the campers trekked for two weeks through that park's rugged mountain wilderness, as well as into Inyo National Forest and Golden Trout Wilderness Area. They slept in meadows, swam in streams, and summited Mt. Whitney, the tallest mountain in the contiguous United States.

How do you spell Tie Sing's name?

Newspaper articles from 1915 spell his name both "Ty Sing" and "Tie Sing"—sometimes on the same page! Horace Albright, who wrote about the trail cook years later, spells the name "Ty Sing," but he gets other campers' names wrong, so I'm not confident about his spelling. For this book I have chosen to use the more common spelling, "Tie Sing."

Courtesy of the National Park Service and the Bancroft Library, University of California, Berkeley, BANC PIC 1954.008-fALB p. 4

Who else went on the trip?

There were nineteen invited guests, two cooks, and a staff of wranglers and packers—about thirty in all. Among that number were some remarkable men.

Courtesy of the Bancroft Library, University of California, Berkeley, 1954:9 Pic

Stephen Mather

Mather made his fortune marketing the mineral borax as a laundry aid. His 20 Mule Team Borax brand is still sold today.

A member of the Sierra Club, Mather was deeply concerned about the lack of oversight in our national parks. Legend says that he wrote an angry letter to the secretary of the interior, Franklin Lane, and that Lane responded, "Dear Steve, if you don't like the way the national parks are run, why don't you come down to Washington and run them yourself?" So Mather did!

When the National Park Service was created in 1916, Mather was named its first head.

Mather felt so strongly that the camping trip was a success that he organized at least two more like it: one in 1916, which Tie Sing also cooked for, and one in 1919, after Tie Sing had died.

Eugene

Tie Sing brought along another Chinese cook, who had also worked for the USGS, as his assistant. We know that his name was Eugene, and a photo survives that shows him working over the stove with Tie Sing. Other than that, we don't know anything about him. He was one of the silent many, including the wranglers who cared for the horses and mules, who brought to life the dreams of better-connected, wealthier men.

Horace Albright

In 1915 Albright had just graduated from Berkeley and was working as Mather's assistant.

Albright's vivid memories of Tie Sing—and of Tie Sing's menus!—were essential to my research. Albright succeeded Mather as the head of the National Park Service.

Frederick Gillett

Gillett was a powerful member of Congress: the ranking Republican in the Appropriations Committee. He had never been in the Sierra Nevada before the camping trip, but afterward, he became one of Mather's most important congressional allies.

Gilbert H. Grosvenor

Grosvenor (pronounced GROVE-nor) was the head of the National Geographic Society. This was his first trip west of Ohio. In April 1916 he devoted an entire issue of *National Geographic* magazine to the national parks. In June, when members of Congress arrived to vote on legislation to create the National Park Service, each found a copy of that issue lying on his desk. That same year, the National Geographic Society helped purchase a tract of land that was then added to Sequoia National Park, near where the Mather Mountain Party had camped.

Grosvenor was a talented photographer. I spent a surprising amount of my research time poring over his vivid photos of the camping trip.

Burton Holmes

Holmes, a filmmaker and lecturer, and his cameraman, Oscar Depue, camped with the group for the first four nights. Holmes annoyed the other campers when he treated them like actors, trying to direct them. After the camping trip Holmes gave public lectures about the Sierra Nevada. Sadly, the footage that Holmes and Depue shot has not survived.

Emerson Hough

Hough (pronounced *HUFF*) loved animals. His writing about the endangered Yellowstone buffalo led to a public outcry that helped save the herd. During the camping trip in this story, one of the horses was injured and had to be killed. The others took the loss in stride, but Hough was deeply saddened.

Hough, unlike the other invited guests, made friends with the hired help. He sometimes traveled during the day with Tie Sing and the mule wranglers instead of with Mather. Albright said that at the end of the trip, "Hough had grown especially fond of [Tie Sing] and with tears in his eyes, parted with his favorite red shirt that [Tie] had taken a fancy to."

Hough wrote about this trip in *Field and Stream* magazine. He also wrote an influential series of articles about the national parks for the *Saturday Evening Post*.

Robert Marshall

At the time of the camping trip, Robert Marshall was chief geographer of the USGS. He had come to know and admire Tie Sing earlier as they camped together on mapping trips in the Sierra Nevada. In 1899 he named Sing Peak in honor of the trail cook. It was Marshall who recommended that Mather hire Tie Sing.

Selected Bibliography

I am deeply indebted to the Bancroft Library at the University of California, Berkeley, for giving me access to the Stephen Tyng Mather Papers. I relied heavily on the library's photos and magazine and newspaper clippings, including *Visalia Daily Times* articles from June through October 1915, such as this one:

Maddox, Ben M., Stephen T. Mather, Frederick H. Gillett, Emerson Hough, Henry Fairfield Osborn, Gilbert H. Grosvenor, Mark Daniels, E. O. McCormick, and Henry Floy. "Noted Men and World Travelers of Mather Party Extol Sierra." *Visalia Daily Times*, July 30, 1915. In Album 1, Stephen Tyng Mather Papers, BANC MSS C-B 535, The Bancroft Library, University of California, Berkeley.

In addition, the following sources were especially helpful:

Albright, Horace Marden, and Robert Cahn. *The Birth of the National Park Service: The Founding Years, 1913–33.* Salt Lake City, UT: Howe Bros., 1985.

Albright, Horace Marden, and Marian Albright Schenk. *Creating the National Park Service: The Missing Years.* Norman, OK: University of Oklahoma Press, 1999. www.nps.gov/parkhistory/online_books/albright2/index.htm

Albright, Horace Marden, and Marian Albright Schenk. *The Mather Mountain Party of 1915: A Full Account of the Adventures of Stephen T. Mather and His Friends in the High Sierra of California.* Three Rivers, CA: Sequoia Natural History Association, 1990.

Chan, Loren B. "The Chinese in Nevada: An Historical Survey, 1856–1970." In *Chinese on the American Frontier*, edited by Arif Dirlik and Malcolm Yeung, 85–122. Lanham, MD: Rowman & Littlefield, 2001. Originally published in the *Nevada Historical Society Quarterly* 25 (Winter 1982): 266–314. www.nsladigitalcollections.org/quarterly#/item/000000071001116/view

Chang, Iris. *The Chinese in America: A Narrative History.* New York: Viking, 2003.

Chung, Sue Fawn. *In Pursuit of Gold: Chinese American Miners and Merchants in the American West.* Urbana, IL: University of Illinois Press, 2011.

Farquhar, Francis Peloubet. *Place Names of the High Sierra.* San Francisco, CA: Sierra Club, 1926. www.yosemite.ca.us/library/place_names_of_the_high_sierra/

Hough, Emerson. *Let Us Go Afield.* New York: D. Appleton, 1916.

Lee, Jennifer 8. "Solving a Riddle Wrapped in a Mystery Inside a Cookie." *New York Times*, January 16, 2008. www.nytimes.com/2008/01/16/dining/16fort.html

Magnaghi, Russell M. "Virginia City's Chinese Community, 1860–1880." In *Chinese on the American Frontier*, edited by Arif Dirlik and Malcolm Yeung, 123–48. Lanham, MD: Rowman & Littlefield, 2001.

Nelson, Clifford M., USGS historian. Email to author. November 9, 2012.

Ramsey, Kristin, and Yenyen Chan. "A Glimpse into Yosemite's Chinese History." National Park Service video, 7:32. December 22, 2011. www.nps.gov/yose/photosmultimedia/chinese.htm

Woodworth, Marshall B. "Who Are Citizens of the United States? Wong Kim Ark Case—Interpretation of Citizenship Clause of Fourteenth Amendment." *American Law Review* 32 (1898): 554–61.

Source Notes

Page 7: "Give [a man] . . . scenery is": Albright, *Creating the National Park Service*, p. 54.

Page 33: "Long may you search the mountains," "Long may you build . . . mountains," and "Where but . . . mountains?" [question mark added]: Albright, *The Mather Mountain Party of 1915*, p. 29.

Page 37: "regarded . . . fine American": Farquhar, p. 149.

Page 38: "Dear Steve, . . . yourself": Albright, *The Birth of the National Park Service*, p. 16, and *Creating the National Park Service*, p. 35.

Page 39: "Hough had . . . fancy to": Albright, *The Mather Mountain Party of 1915*, p. 30.